William Sim
My ZODIAC
Colouring Book

A sophisticated activity book

mc Marshall Cavendish
Editions

Introduction

My Zodiac Colouring Book features the animals of the Chinese Zodiac. Each year is represented by one of 12 animals in a repeating cycle. The sequence is as follows: Rat, Ox, Tiger, Rabbit, Dragon, Snake, Horse, Goat, Monkey, Rooster, Dog and Pig. The Chinese Lunar Calendar differs from the Gregorian Calendar which starts on 1 January as it includes leap months, so in some years there are 13 months. Based on this, the Lunar New Year is a moving date in January or February.

Chinese Zodiac Signs

Rat:	1948, 1960, 1972, 1984, 1996, 2008, 2020
Ox:	1949, 1961, 1973, 1985, 1997, 2009, 2021
Tiger:	1950, 1962, 1974, 1986, 1998, 2010, 2022
Rabbit:	1951, 1963, 1975, 1987, 1999, 2011, 2023
Dragon:	1952, 1964, 1976, 1988, 2000, 2012, 2024
Snake:	1953, 1965, 1977, 1989, 2001, 2013, 2025
Horse:	1954, 1966, 1978, 1990, 2002, 2014, 2026
Goat:	1955, 1967, 1979, 1991, 2003, 2015, 2027
Monkey:	1956, 1968, 1980, 1992, 2004, 2016, 2028
Rooster:	1957, 1969, 1981, 1993, 2005, 2017, 2029
Dog:	1958, 1970, 1982, 1994, 2006, 2018, 2030
Pig:	1959, 1971, 1983, 1995, 2007, 2019, 2031

About the Author

William Sim's art often portrays a fantasy world in a kaleidoscope of candy hues and shades. The subjects, a blend of nature and mechanical objects, collaborate individually and collectively to depict dreamscapes of immense optimism. Branding himself as the Merchant of Happiness, William is a full-time art practitioner and a partner at a visual arts studio based in Singapore since 1997. He has showcased his paintings in various group and solo exhibitions in Singapore and countries like South Korea, Taiwan and Hong Kong.

William has also authored three other colouring books, two books of colouring postcards, an illustrated book on fauna titled *Botanical Singapore* and a travel book introducing the sights of the country titled *Out and About in Singapore*.

Readers are invited to share their masterpieces on Instagram #colouringthelioncity

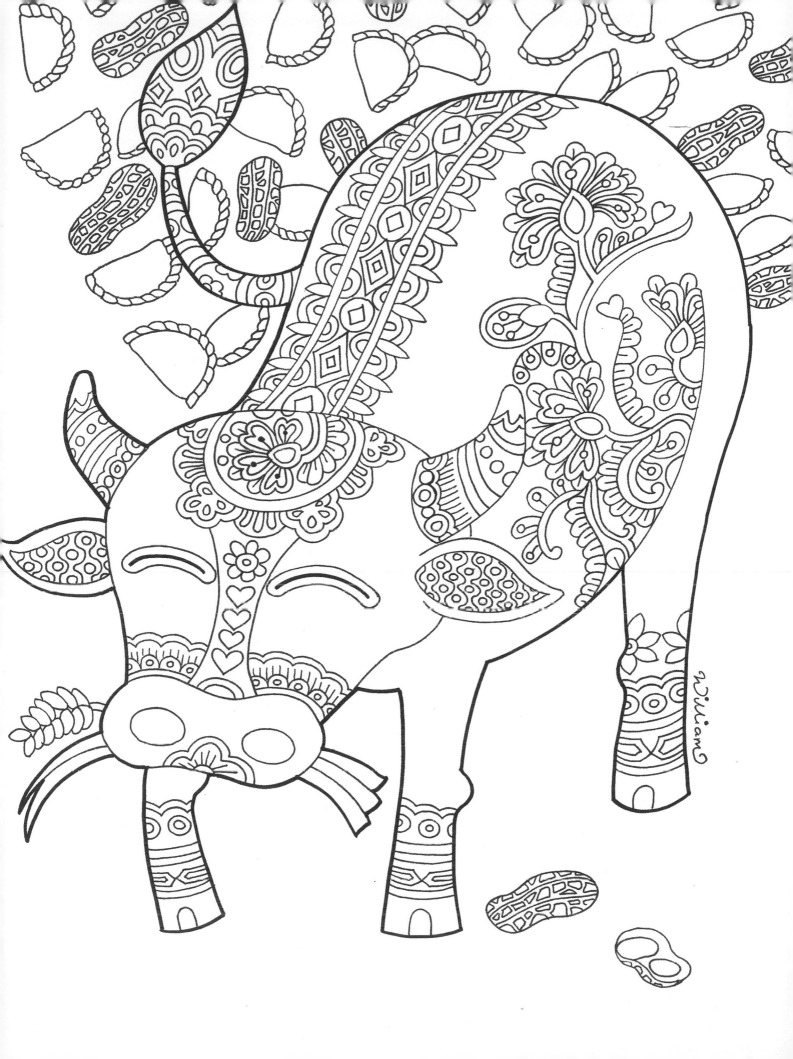

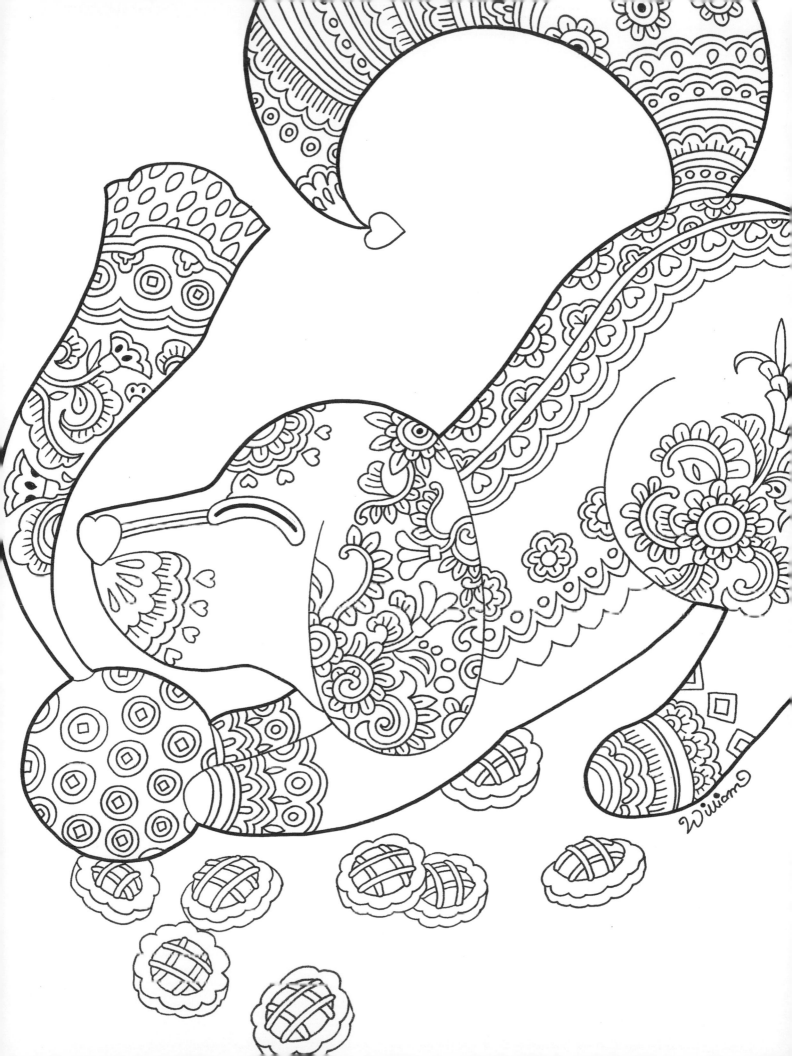

William

William

© 2022 William Sim and Marshall Cavendish International (Asia) Private Limited

Published by Marshall Cavendish Editions
An imprint of Marshall Cavendish International

Other Marshall Cavendish Offices
Marshall Cavendish Corporation, 800 Westchester Ave, Suite N-641, Rye Brook, NY 10573, USA • Marshall Cavendish International (Thailand) Co Ltd, 253 Asoke, 16th Floor, Sukhumvit 21 Road, Klongtoey Nua, Wattana, Bangkok 10110, Thailand • Marshall Cavendish (Malaysia) Sdn Bhd, Times Subang, Lot 46, Subang Hi-Tech Industrial Park, Batu Tiga, 40000 Shah Alam, Selangor Darul Ehsan, Malaysia

Marshall Cavendish is a trademark of Times Publishing Limited.

ISBN: 978 981 5009 45 3

Printed in Singapore